RAINY DAYS

KITES

AND FLYING OBJECTS

DENNY ROBSON

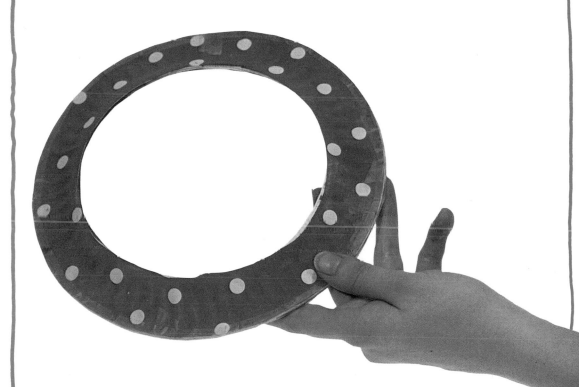

FRANKLIN WATTS
LONDON · NEW YORK · TORONTO · SYDNEY

CONTENTS

Design: David West
Children's Book Design
Designer: Flick Killerby
Photography: Roger Vlitos
Editor: Denny Robson

© Aladdin Books Ltd 1991

Created and designed by
N.W. Books Ltd
28 Percy Street
London W1P 9FF

First published in
Great Britain in 1991 by
Franklin Watts Ltd
96 Leonard Street
London EC2A 4RH

ISBN 0 7496 0614 2

A CIP catalogue record for this book
is available from the British Library

Introduction

All of the projects in this book are designed to fly in one way or another. You will find some quite simple to make, like the paper dart or the frisbee. Others, like the kites, require more skill and perhaps the help of an older person.

When it comes to making the objects fly, don't be put off if things don't go right first time. You may have to experiment a little with angles, weights or strings before achieving the perfect flight. But this is all part of the fun!

You will need space for your flying objects. A garden or the park is the best place for many of them. Make sure you read the warning on page 32 before flying your kites.

Here are some of the materials used to make the projects in this book. Most things are not expensive to buy and you may find much of what you need at home. Before you start, gather together all the things you need and read the instructions through once or twice. If the project involves paint or glue, cover your work surface with newspaper.

Paper plane

Paper planes are quick and easy to make. Yet they can be spectacular flying craft, accurate and fast. There are endless designs for paper planes and many simply involve the careful folding of a single sheet of paper. Try experimenting with your own designs. Cut out wings, trim the tail or weight the nose until you have lift off!

1 Take a rectangular sheet of stiff paper and make the first fold as shown. Unfold.

1

2 Take the folded corner across to the opposite side and make the second fold. Unfold.

2

3 Open out the sheet of paper. Fold across the middle point of the two creases.

3

4 Using the creases as your guide, fold in the two sides so that you are left with this triangle shape.

4

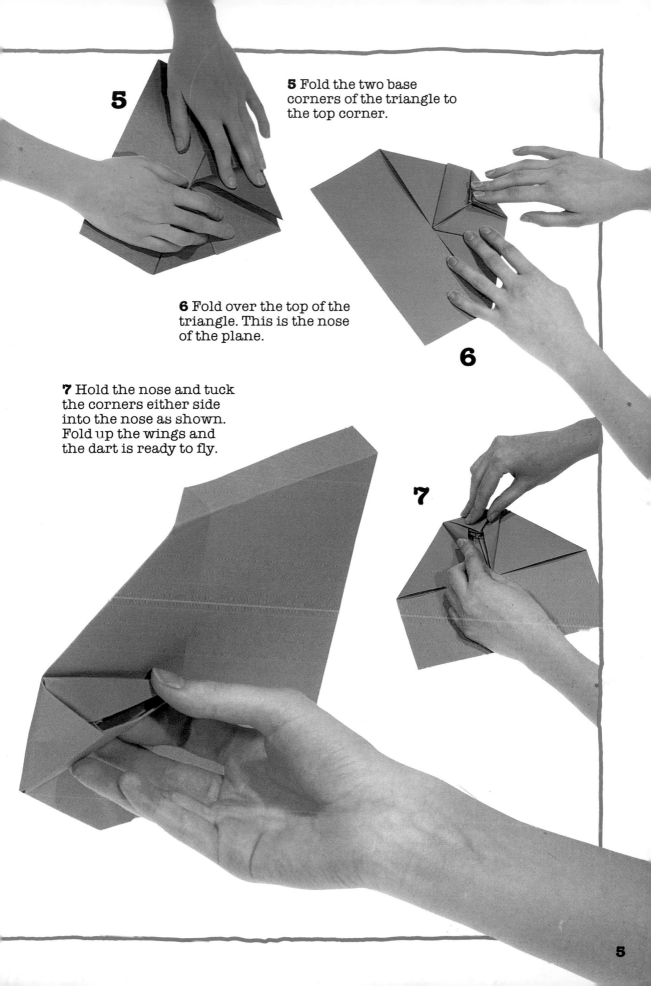

5 Fold the two base corners of the triangle to the top corner.

6 Fold over the top of the triangle. This is the nose of the plane.

7 Hold the nose and tuck the corners either side into the nose as shown. Fold up the wings and the dart is ready to fly.

Helicopter

This clever little object twirls up into the air, spinning like the propeller of a helicopter.

You will need two plastic drinking straws, card, sticky tape and scissors.

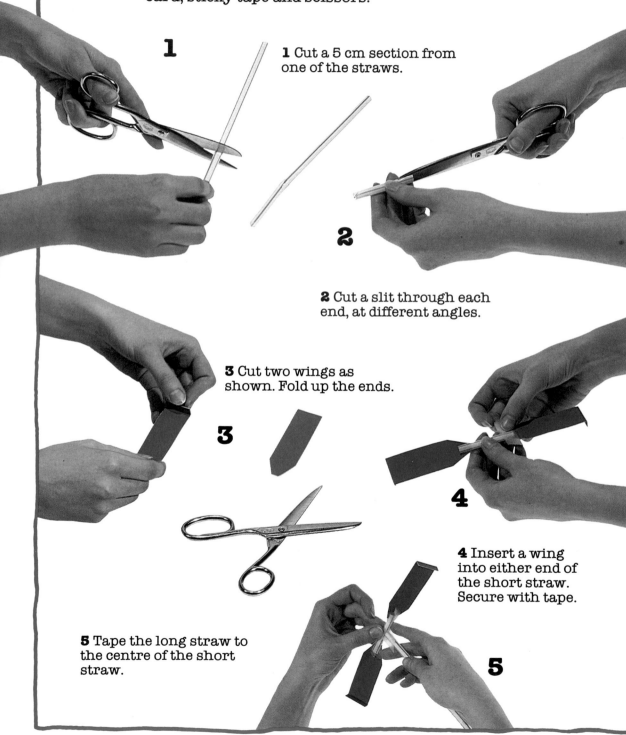

1

1 Cut a 5 cm section from one of the straws.

2

2 Cut a slit through each end, at different angles.

3 Cut two wings as shown. Fold up the ends.

3

4

4 Insert a wing into either end of the short straw. Secure with tape.

5 Tape the long straw to the centre of the short straw.

5

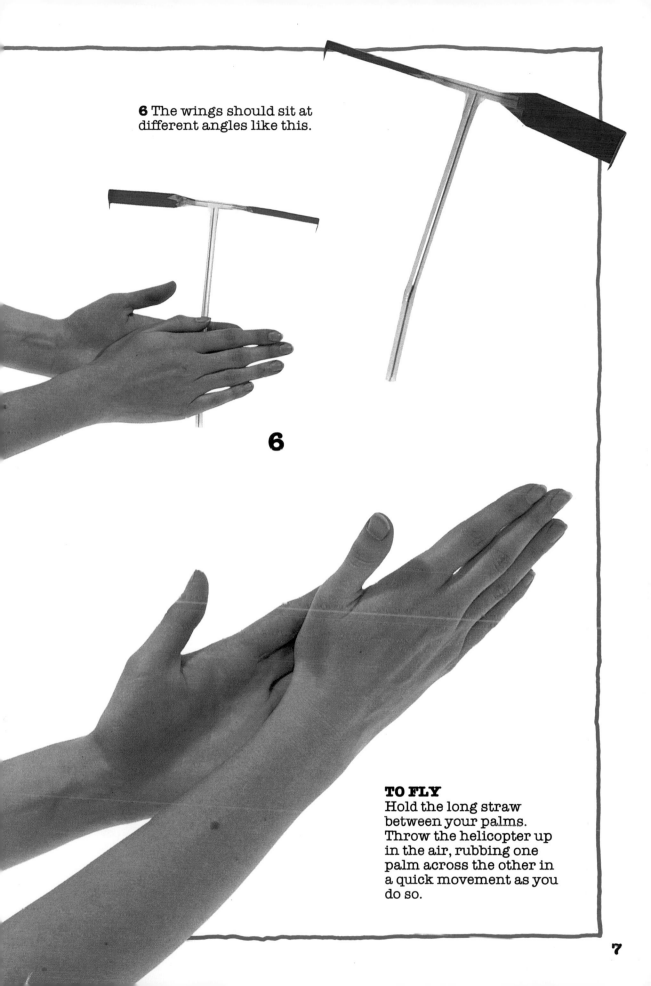

6 The wings should sit at different angles like this.

6

TO FLY
Hold the long straw between your palms. Throw the helicopter up in the air, rubbing one palm across the other in a quick movement as you do so.

Balloon rocket

This balloon rocket is great fun. It whizzes along a string at top speed.

You will need a long balloon, drinking straw, sticky tape, bulldog clip, string (at least three metres), card, coloured pencils and scissors.

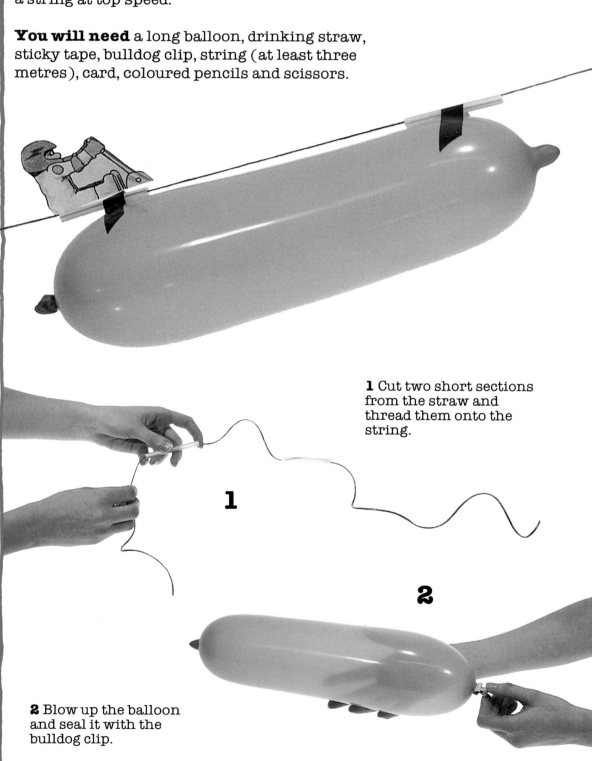

1 Cut two short sections from the straw and thread them onto the string.

2 Blow up the balloon and seal it with the bulldog clip.

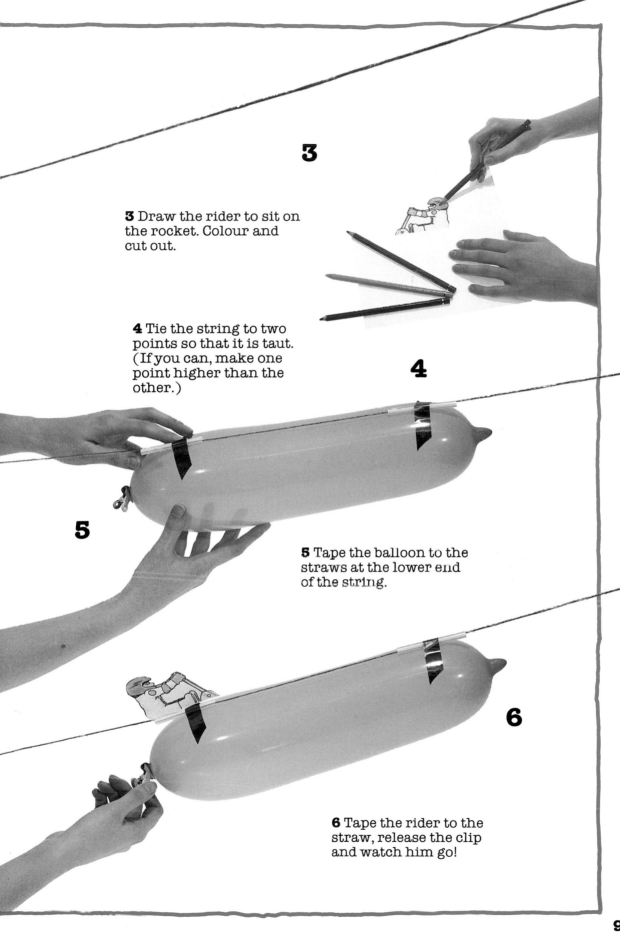

3

3 Draw the rider to sit on the rocket. Colour and cut out.

4 Tie the string to two points so that it is taut. (If you can, make one point higher than the other.)

4

5

5 Tape the balloon to the straws at the lower end of the string.

6

6 Tape the rider to the straw, release the clip and watch him go!

Parachute

This brightly coloured parachute is actually made from a dustbin liner!

You will need a dustbin liner, coloured tape, string, a small toy and scissors.

1 Cut a square, about 30cm × 30cm, from the dustbin liner.

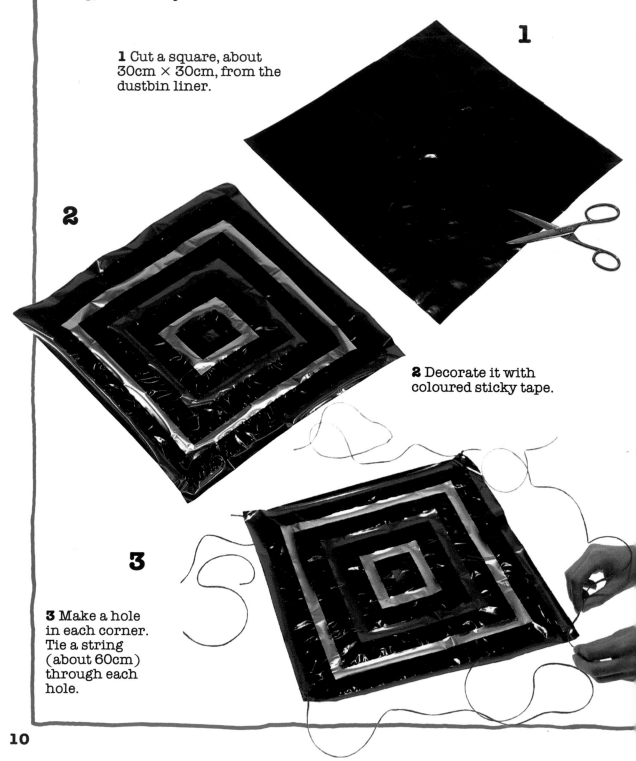

1

2

2 Decorate it with coloured sticky tape.

3

3 Make a hole in each corner. Tie a string (about 60cm) through each hole.

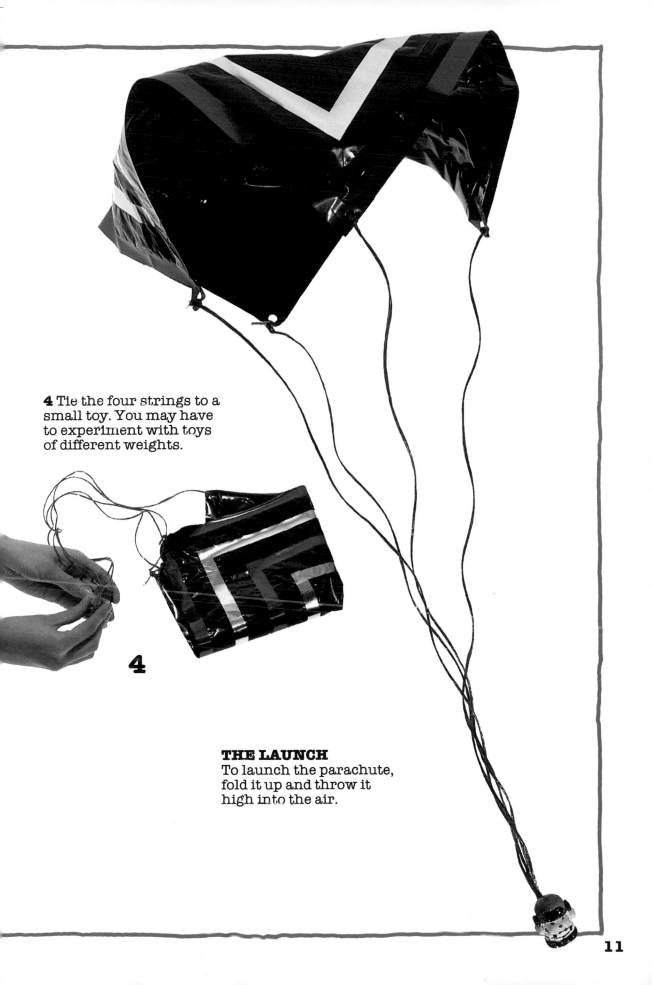

4 Tie the four strings to a
small toy. You may have
to experiment with toys
of different weights.

4

THE LAUNCH
To launch the parachute,
fold it up and throw it
high into the air.

Blow dart

You can organise an exciting contest with this project. Get together with friends and each make a dart in your own colours. Take your marks, and see whose dart travels furthest!

You will need a drinking straw, card, paper, paper clip, sticky tape, coloured pencils, scissors.

1 Cut one small and one large triangle from the card. (The straw needs to be longer than the height of the large triangle.)

1

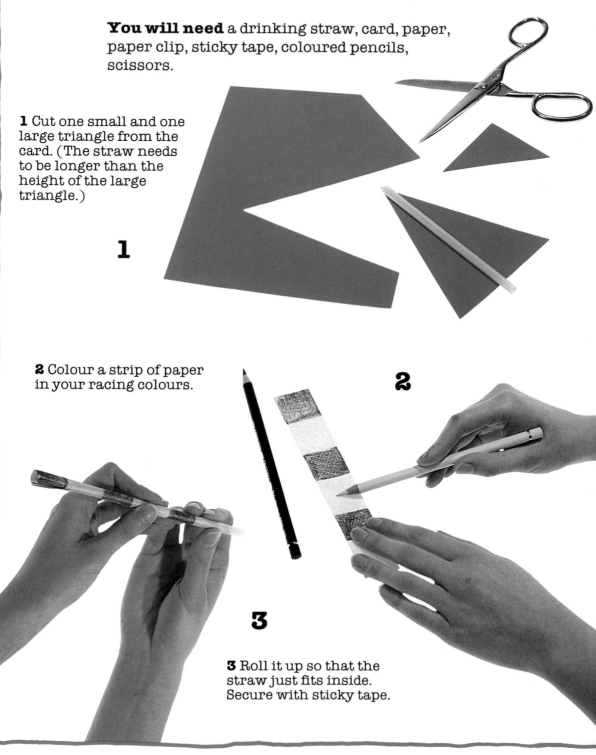

2 Colour a strip of paper in your racing colours.

2

3

3 Roll it up so that the straw just fits inside. Secure with sticky tape.

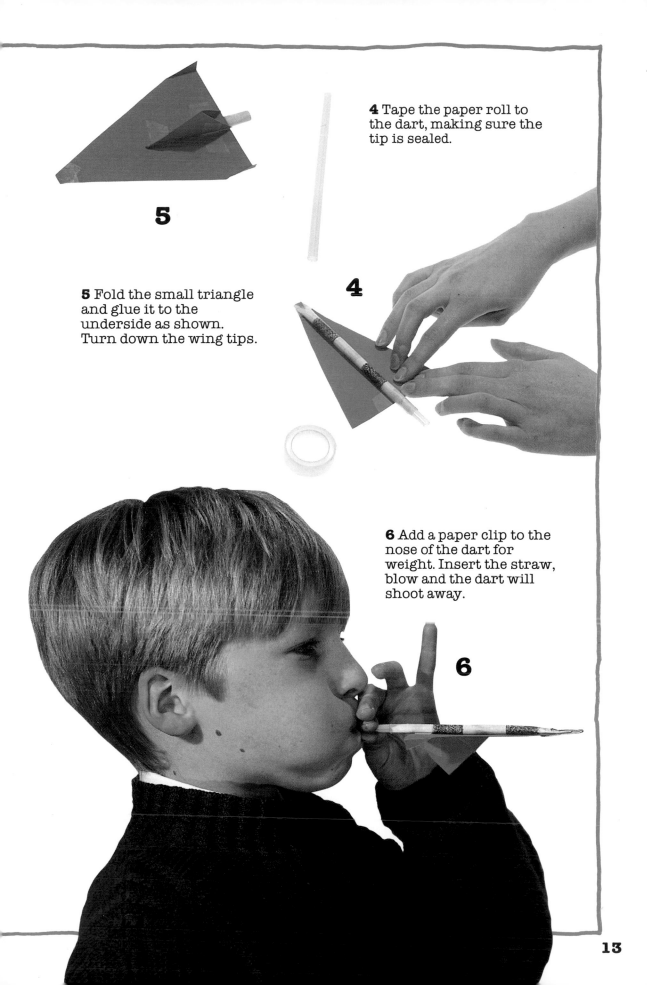

5

5 Fold the small triangle
and glue it to the
underside as shown.
Turn down the wing tips.

4 Tape the paper roll to
the dart, making sure the
tip is sealed.

4

6 Add a paper clip to the
nose of the dart for
weight. Insert the straw,
blow and the dart will
shoot away.

6

Frisbee

Frisbee throwing is a great game. Once you've mastered the technique, you'll be surprised at how far the frisbee can travel.

You will need four paper plates, scissors, gummed shapes, glue, paint and a paintbrush.

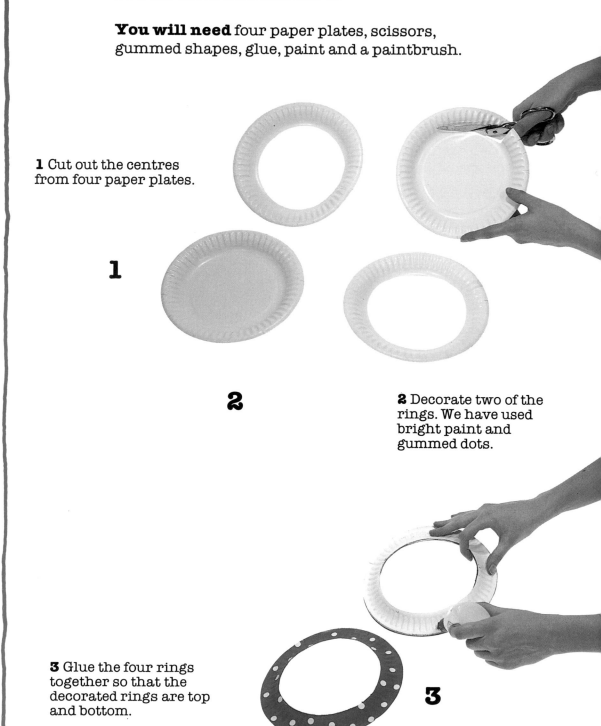

1 Cut out the centres from four paper plates.

1

2

2 Decorate two of the rings. We have used bright paint and gummed dots.

3 Glue the four rings together so that the decorated rings are top and bottom.

3

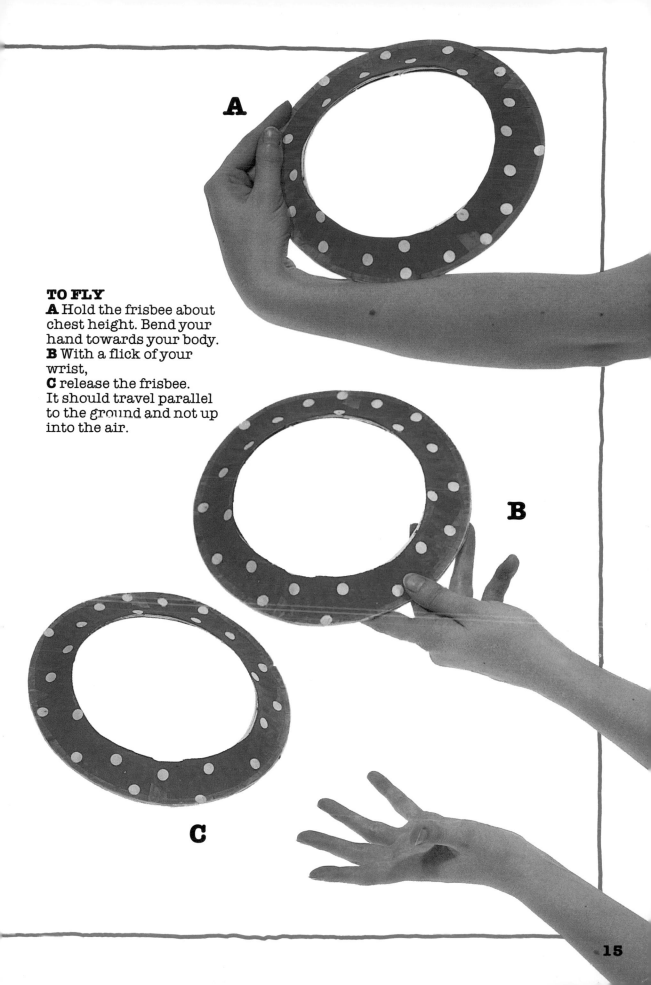

A

TO FLY
A Hold the frisbee about chest height. Bend your hand towards your body.
B With a flick of your wrist,
C release the frisbee. It should travel parallel to the ground and not up into the air.

B

C

Traditional kite

Kite flying was probably invented in the East, more than 2,000 years ago. This simple kite will fly in the slightest of winds.

You will need a plastic bag, 2 light garden canes, string, strong tape, kite cord and spindle, paints and paint brush.

1 Cut this shape from a plastic bag.

1

2 Cut the cane to fit the kite. Cross as shown and tie at the centre. These are the struts.

3

3 Tape the struts to the kite. Turn the kite over and put a piece of tape over the point at which the struts cross.

2

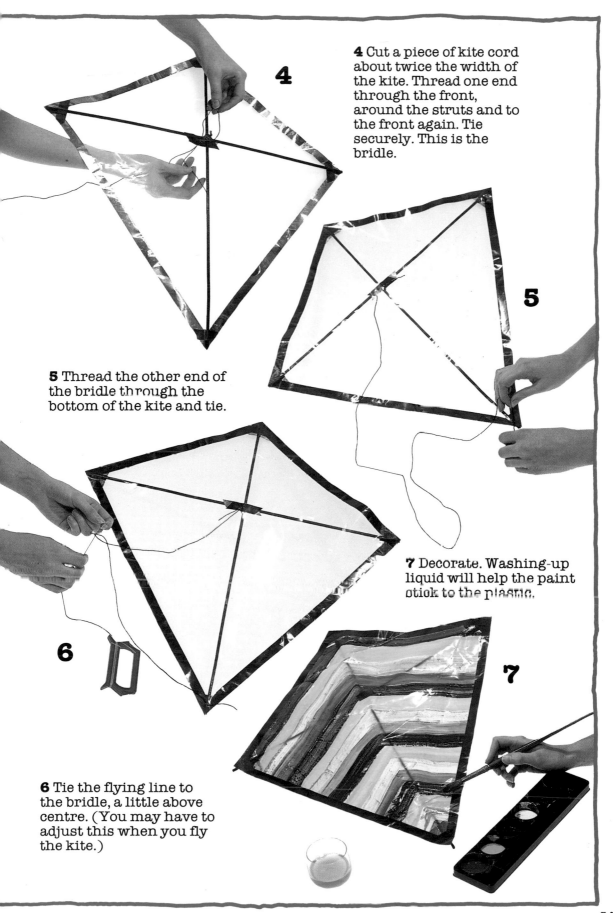

4 Cut a piece of kite cord about twice the width of the kite. Thread one end through the front, around the struts and to the front again. Tie securely. This is the bridle.

5 Thread the other end of the bridle through the bottom of the kite and tie.

7 Decorate. Washing-up liquid will help the paint stick to the plastic.

6 Tie the flying line to the bridle, a little above centre. (You may have to adjust this when you fly the kite.)

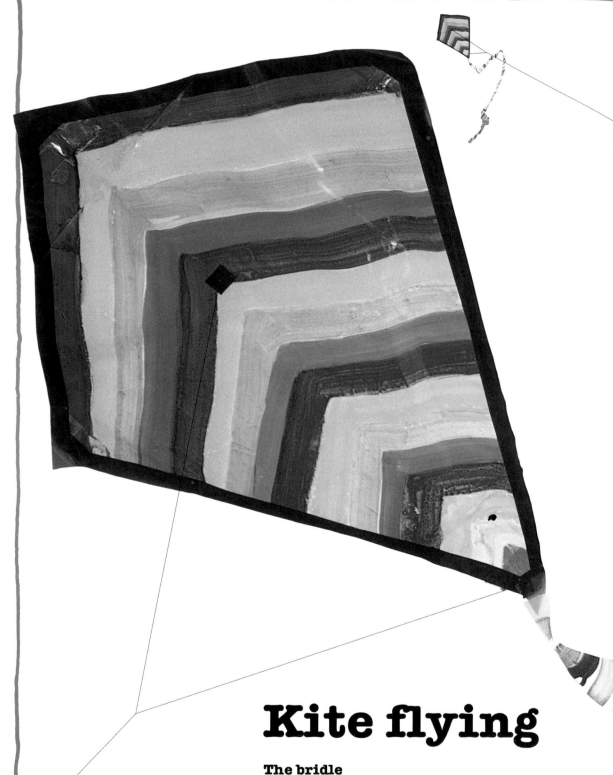

Kite flying

The bridle
The short strings from the kite to the flying line are called the bridle. They hold the kite at the correct angle to the wind.

HOW TO FLY A KITE

To launch the kite, unwind about 20 metres of line. Get a friend to hold the kite above his head, with the tail behind him.

When the kite is up in the air, pull down on the line to get more height. Work the line so that the kite leans forward into the wind.

As he releases the kite, you walk backwards until the kite begins to rise. Then gradually let out more line.

The tail

A tail gives the kite stability. Make it out of plastic (about five times the height of the kite). Decorate and tape it to the bottom of the kite.

Clown kite

This clown kite doesn't need a tail. The hole in its mouth gives it the stability it needs. The shape is important, so turn to page 32 for the proportions.

You will need plastic, strong tape, garden canes, kite cord and spindle, scissors, paints and paint brush.

1 Cut out the shape of the kite according to the proportions on page 32. Tape the edges.

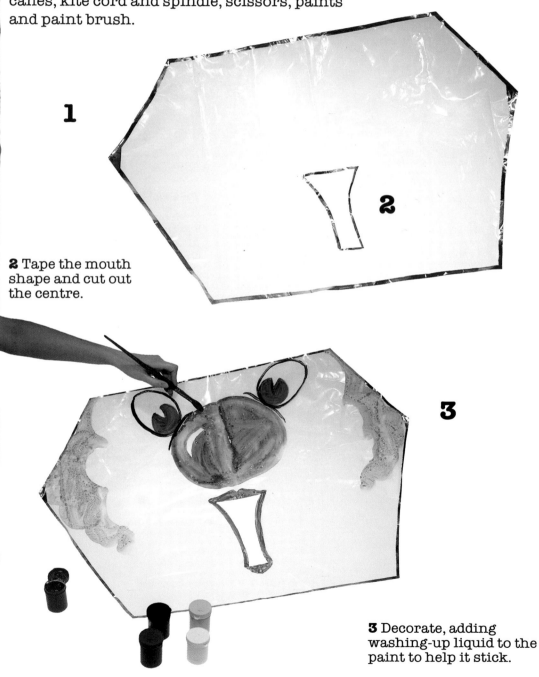

1

2

2 Tape the mouth shape and cut out the centre.

3

3 Decorate, adding washing-up liquid to the paint to help it stick.

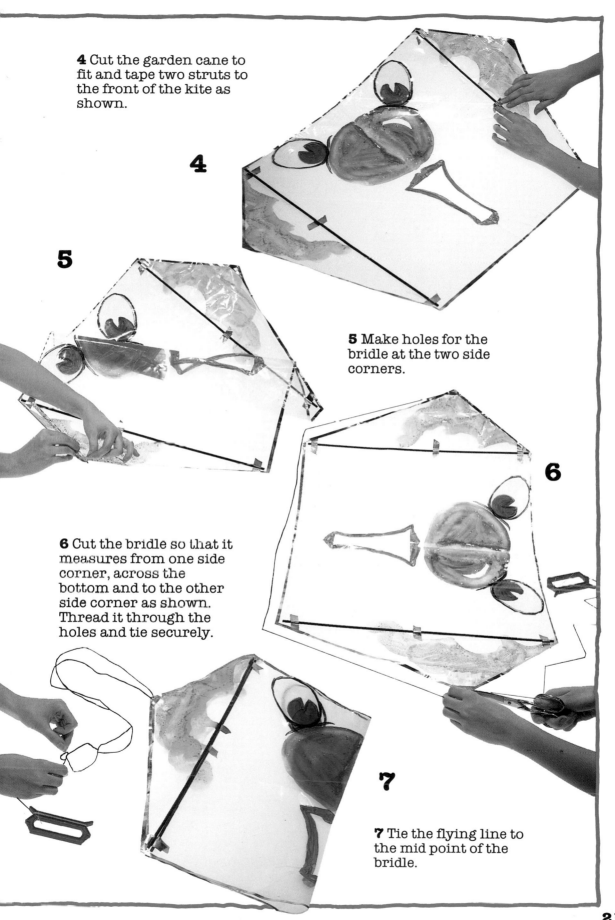

4 Cut the garden cane to fit and tape two struts to the front of the kite as shown.

4

5

5 Make holes for the bridle at the two side corners.

6

6 Cut the bridle so that it measures from one side corner, across the bottom and to the other side corner as shown. Thread it through the holes and tie securely.

7

7 Tie the flying line to the mid point of the bridle.

Flying the clown

You may have to experiment to see which of
your kites fly best in different kinds of weather.
This clown kite will fly well in either a strong or
a light wind.

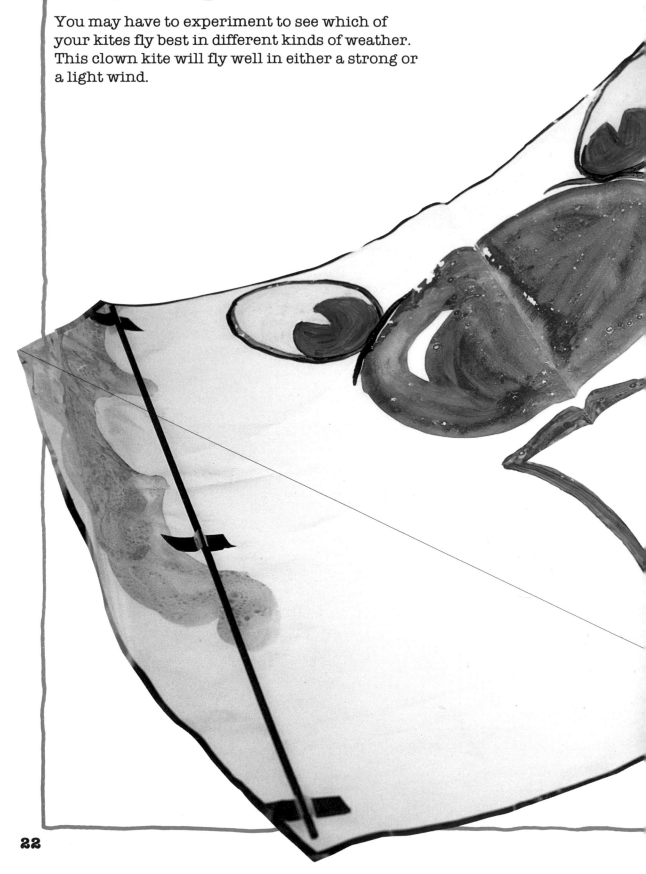

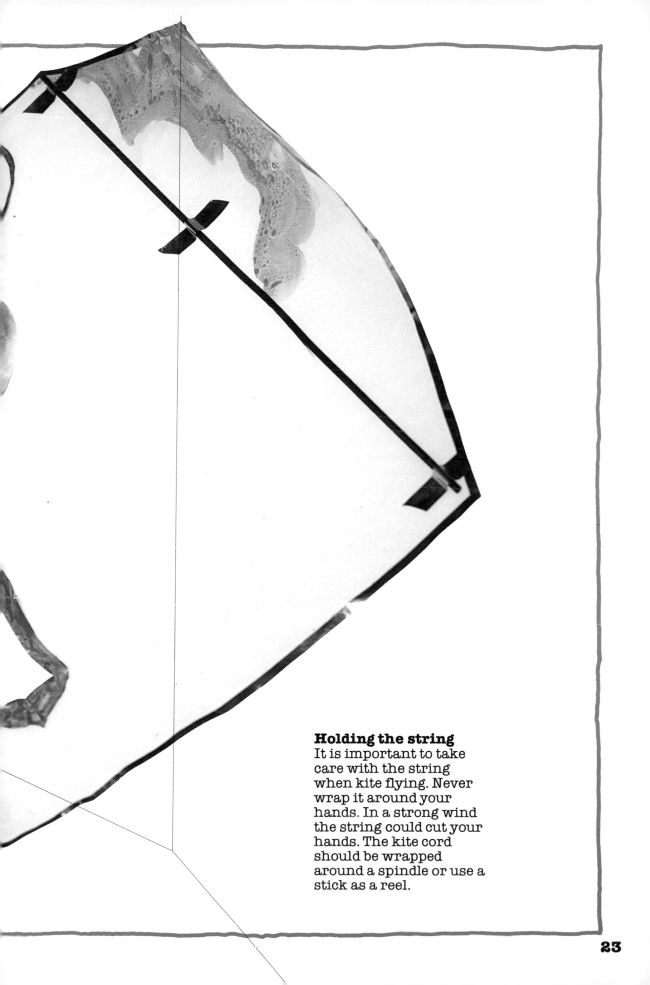

Holding the string
It is important to take care with the string when kite flying. Never wrap it around your hands. In a strong wind the string could cut your hands. The kite cord should be wrapped around a spindle or use a stick as a reel.

Square kite

This unusual kite is based on a Korean fighting kite. (When true fighting kites are flown, the object is to sever an opponent's kite string!)

You will need garden cane, strong sticky tape, bin liner, kite cord and spindle, gummed shapes.

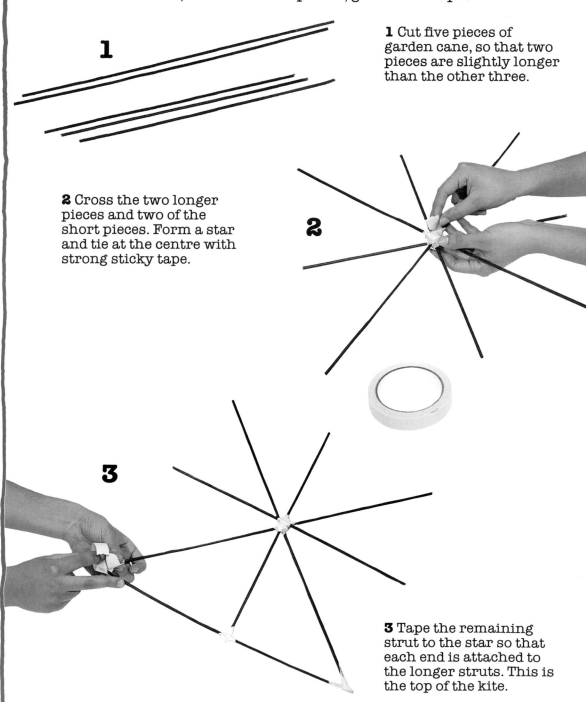

1 Cut five pieces of garden cane, so that two pieces are slightly longer than the other three.

2 Cross the two longer pieces and two of the short pieces. Form a star and tie at the centre with strong sticky tape.

3 Tape the remaining strut to the star so that each end is attached to the longer struts. This is the top of the kite.

4 Lay the frame on the bin liner. Draw a square to fit and cut out. Lay the frame on the square and draw a shape at the centre as shown. Cut out. Tape each strut to the plastic.

4

5

5 Turn the kite over. Cut three pieces of kite cord, about the length of one of the sides of the square.
  Tie one piece to each of the top corners and the third to the bottom at the centre.

6

6 Tie the ends of the cords together. This is the bridle. Tie the kite string to the bridle. Decorate the kite with gummed shapes.

Flying the square kite

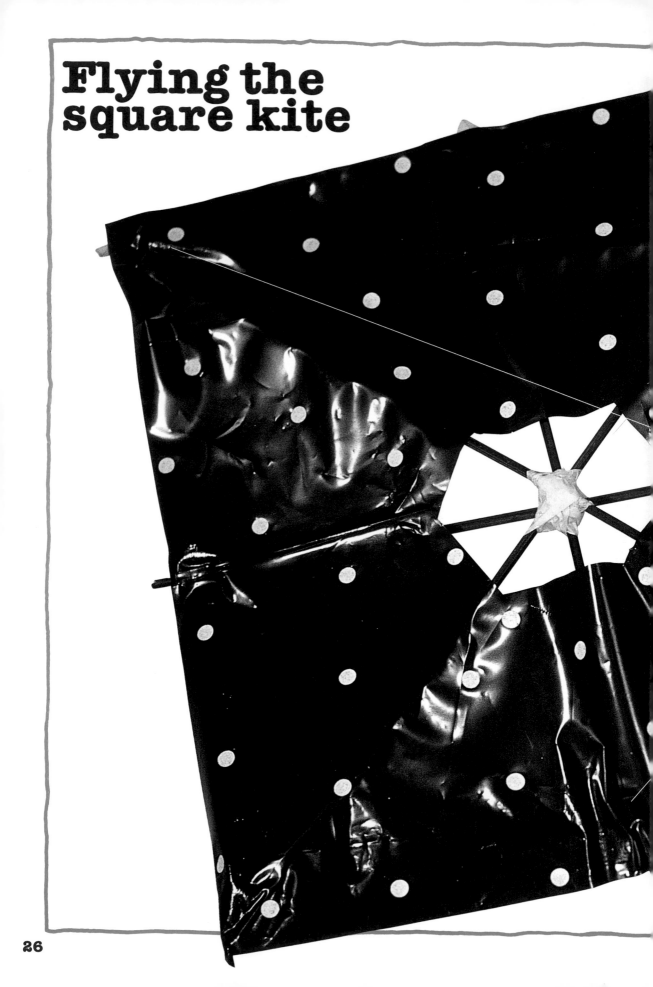

There is a lot of trial and error in kite flying. You have to be prepared to make adjustments to your kites or even change one kite for another, depending on the strength of the wind.

Like the clown kite, the hole in the centre of this square kite gives it stability and so it doesn't need a tail.

Triangle kite

The triangle kite is a box kite. Box kites have side surfaces which give them stability. Unlike the other kites, the triangle kite needs no bridle.

You will need garden cane, strong sticky tape, bin liner, double-sided sticky tape, gummed shapes, kite cord and spindle.

1 Cut three long pieces of garden cane and six shorter pieces.

2 Form two triangles with the shorter lengths of cane. Tape the corners with strong sticky tape.

3 Tape the long struts to the two triangles as shown.

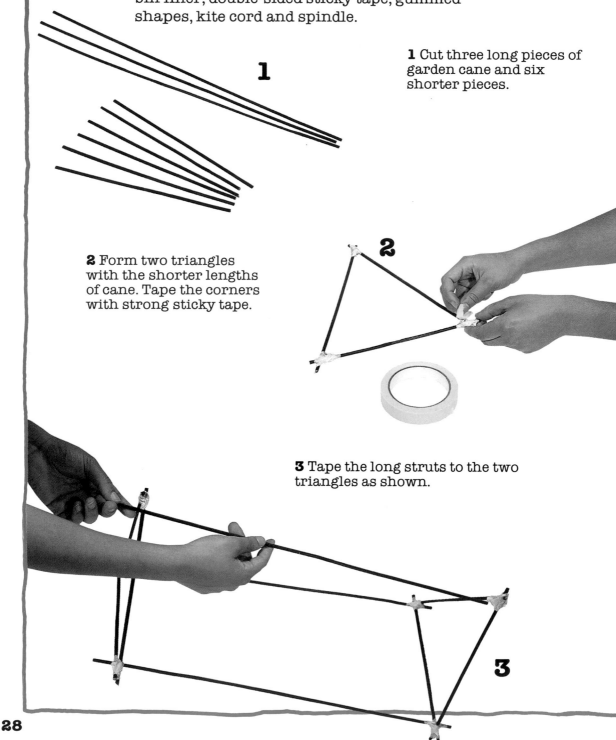

4 Cut two strips from the dustbin liner.
The strips should be long enough to
wrap around the frame (see below),
and wide enough to cover about one
third of its length.

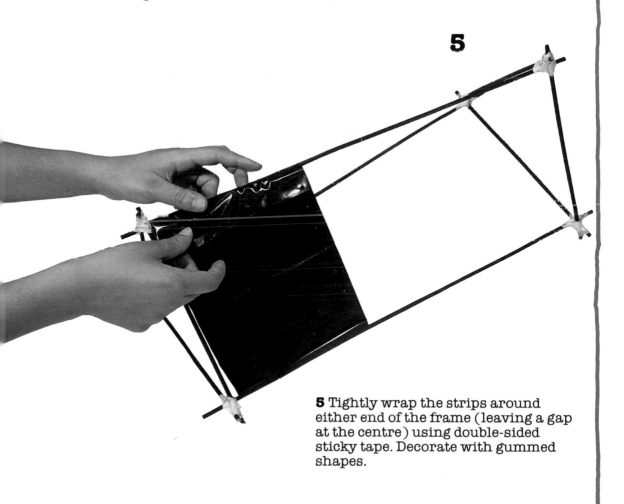

5 Tightly wrap the strips around
either end of the frame (leaving a gap
at the centre) using double-sided
sticky tape. Decorate with gummed
shapes.

Flying the triangle kite

This is a good kite to fly in heavy winds because it will be stable even in gusty conditions. It should fly edge-on to the wind. The front two surfaces provide stability and the back surface gives the kite lift.

WARNING!

Always take care when flying your kites. Never fly your kites near overhead power lines, near a road or railway, near an airport or in a thunderstorm.

The best place to choose is an open area of parkland away from trees, the windy side of a hill or at the seaside.

Clown kite

Use these proportions for the clown kite. It can be made any size you want.

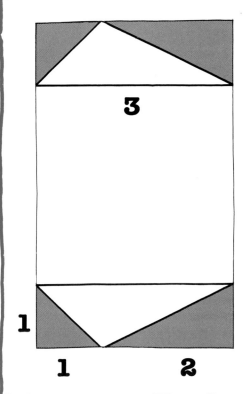

Index